LITTLE BANKERS

Aldric Anthony Fishe

About the Author

Aldric Anthony Fishe was born in Hempstead, New York, on November 1, 1962.
He is the youngest of four children born to James and Toni Fishe. Aldric and his three siblings share an older brother born to his father, James. The family moved to Amityville, New York, until 1973, when the family moved to North Carolina. From a young age, Aldric always loved to draw and dreamed of becoming an animator. He also had a dream of owning a business. In 1981 Aldric joined the United States Air Force and served for four honorable years. During his military service, Aldric spent time in the Philippines where he met his wife, Debbie. He and Debbie married on January 16, 1986. And through their bond, they had two children, Tempestt and Tamica. Aldric and Debbie now have three grandsons. In 1990 Aldric graduated from Catawba Valley Community College with a degree in Graphic Art & Design. Aldric tried many different businesses throughout his childhood and adulthood. Many of his ideas failed, but he found success through hard work and passion. He now owns three businesses,

one being a Graphics Company. In 2022 Aldric retired from the North Carolina Department of Correction after 20 years of service. He now spends his days running his businesses and enjoying his grandchildren.

Dedication

This book is dedicated to

James K. Fishe
Anthony (Toni) Fishe
James Michael Fishe
Geneva Goforth
Ruth Baskerville
Charles L. Daniel
And to all the Entrepreneurs, young and old, who have the imagination to dream and the audacity to make those dreams come true.

Acknowledgment

I would like to thank Debbie Young for all her help with this book. Her help with the text and giving me feedback were invaluable. I would also like to thank Debbie Fishe, Tempestt Virgil, Tamica Whaley, Marshall Reid, and Clifton Coulter for all their support during the development of this book.

Table of Contents

Chapter One - The Beginning

In the summer of 1972, I was a wild-eyed 9-year-old boy living in an all-black neighborhood in Amityville on Long Island, New York. I was the youngest of the four children born to James and Toni Fishe; there was my oldest sister Debbie, my brother Michael, my sister Stephanie and myself, Aldric. Oh, and I can't forget my oldest brother, Ricky, who shared the same father but had a different mother from my siblings and me. Ricky lived with his mother in North Carolina and would visit us almost every summer.

Amityville is the place famous for the real-life movie "The Amityville Horror." All the businesses in the section of Amityville that we lived in were black-owned and operated. There was a gas station, a cab company, a pharmacy, a dentist, the pharmacist's brother, and a barbershop.

Growing up around black-owned and operated businesses profoundly affected my self-esteem and drive to own a business. It is where I first gained my entrepreneurial spirit; on the other hand, it is also where I first experienced the wrong side of making money. I observed guys shoot dice on the corner. I witnessed my parents play illegal numbers games, as well as my father's Saturday night poker games (which almost always ended in a crazy fight). I would see guys riding around the neighborhood in nice cars and wearing fancy clothes. But, even at my young age, I knew they didn't get those things by singing in the church choir. Making money was important for life and survival, even if a person had to break the rules.

I decided to start my first business, a lemonade stand. I found a few pieces of old wood and two crates and built the frame; soon, I was charging five cents for a nice cold glass. If lemonade was unavailable—meaning I couldn't afford the lemons—there was Plan B: Kool-Aid! You could buy ten Kool-Aid packs for a dollar. Now that was a bargain. Occasionally, I sold a few pieces of candy whenever I could get my hands on some. The mailman was my best customer. He was a tall thin white man, and now that I think about it, he was the only person who worked in our neighborhood that wasn't black. He would walk up to my stand carrying his mailbag full of mail, and sweat would drip from his face. He would reach in his pocket, drop a nickel down on the counter, and I would pour him a glass. Usually, before he finished the first glass, he would drop another nickel down for a second one.

It felt good making money, and soon I had the fever. To me, making money was the best thing since Saturday morning cartoons! My family was not poor, but at the same time, we were far from wealthy. And for a black family in the early seventies, that was a blessing. Don't get me wrong; my mother and father struggled most of the time and worked hard to put food on the table and clothes on our backs. We were no strangers to hand-me-down clothing or yard sales. When we came in from school, we had to take off our "school clothes" and put on our "play clothes." I often saw my mother and father sitting at the kitchen table, trying to figure out how to pay all the bills. The look on their faces at that table would stay with me for the rest of my life. I decided to work hard to have a business so I wouldn't struggle. But I learned later that childhood dreams don't always become adult realities.

Although I loved my little side hustle, my brother Michael and I would find time to hang out with our friends—and let me tell you, this would often end in some mischief. If you have never lived in a black neighborhood in the North, you may not relate to what goes on there.

Let me tell you about our antics with Mr. Carter. Mr. Carter owned and operated the gas station up on Greatneck Road. Back in those days, all gas stations were full-service. That means the attendant would put gas in your car, check the oil, and wash your windshield. A long black cord usually ran from the front of the gas station to the pumps. When a car ran over it, a bell would ring to let the attendant know someone was out there. My brother Michael and I, along with our friend Steven Hicks, would ride our bikes back and forth over that black cord, causing the bell to ring. Mr. Carter would run out of the office thinking he had a customer. But, when he saw us, he would yell, "If you damn kids don't get the hell out of here, I'm gonna bust your heads." We would ride round and round, making the bell ring! Mr. Carter would chase us as we sped away in amusement. All three of us were lucky he could never identify us.

One time Michael, Steven, and I had the great idea of making money cutting grass. We used an old lawnmower Steven had at his house. It was all rusted, and if you wanted to start it, you had to turn a wind-up metal crank on top of the motor. You had to wind it until it stopped and hit a lever that would turn the engine.

Stevens's older brother Sam would say, "You guys are crazy if you think that's going to work." Sam was about 17 and told us it wouldn't work every time we attempted something. We walked to the gas station with a quart can and asked Mr. Carter for a nickel's worth of gas. The price of gasoline at that time was thirty-six cents a gallon. Therefore, a nickel's worth was enough for us to fill the lawn mower tank. Mr. Carter would fold his arms, and with a look of aggravation, he would ask, "Five cents worth?"

"Yes," answered Micheal.

Then, with a great sigh, Mr. Carter would grab the handle and pump a nickel's worth of gas into the can. We were so bold that we didn't even worry about him recognizing us from the many times we terrorized him by ringing the station bell.

Sam was right in this case; we never got the lawn mower started, and our business cutting grass ended before it started. But I still had that fire in my belly to make money. I learned later in life that running a business and dealing with the public is demanding. After running several companies, I now understand how Mr.

Carter felt when we drove him nuts by ringing that bell. But we were kids, and kids do boneheaded things.

That summer, my family and I went to North Carolina to visit Grandma Ozell. Grandma Ozell was my father's mother, and we always looked forward to visiting her. Being from New York, my siblings and I loved to see how the so-called country people lived and compare our differences in culture and accents. We would find humor in the people's southern drawl. Little did we realize that what goes around comes around. My northern friends can now attest that I have obtained a southern drawl.

My mother and father were both born and raised in North Carolina. My dad was born in Catawba County, and my mom in Lincoln County; they met at Tuckers Campground. If you have never experienced a camp meeting, you have missed out on an adventure. People would sleep in these wooden "tents." These tents did not have traditional floors but floors made of straw and dirt.

Another thing I remember is that there weren't any functional toilets, and people kept buckets in the tents, and that's where you did your business. It sounds gross now that I think about it, but to a boy in the 70s who was used to city living, it was indeed an experience.

During the camp meeting, the focus was on church. There was an arbor on the grounds where they would have revival services every night. People had stands there where you could purchase food, and fish and country ham sandwiches were the most popular. There were photo booths, as well as cotton candy, candy apples, and all sorts of treats for the kids. Children from different counties would come together to play, and adults would mingle with friends and family that they hadn't seen in a long time. The camp meeting was something the black community looked forward to every year! I was fascinated by the food stands, and they helped fuel my desire to run a business. The campground was one of the few places I saw black people running businesses in the south. Don't get me wrong, there were blacks running companies in North Carolina, but I never saw so many black entrepreneurs in one place.

While living in Amityville, my mom and dad always talked about moving the family back "home". Although we just brushed it off as wishful thinking, we found out during our trip to see Grandma Ozell in 1972 that they were serious about it. One morning my brother Michael and I were awakened by the sound of a bulldozer. We got dressed and ran outside to see the field beside our grandmother's house cleared by the bulldozers. If we had any doubt about moving to North Carolina, it was removed by what we were witnessing. We had no idea our parents had planned to begin the construction of a house on this trip. My siblings and I were excited—but at the same time, we were sad because we would have to leave our friends in New York. For their part, my parents tried to cushion the blow by promising us that they would buy us new bikes and other toys.

By June of 1973, the contractors had finished building the house, and we were planning to move by August to start school in September. My father hired a moving company to transport all our belongings, and I tearfully said goodbye to all my friends in the neighborhood. By now, the reality of moving had set in, and I was a bit sad. But at the same time, I was looking forward to the next chapter in my life. We met a few friends on our yearly summer visits to see our grandmother; therefore, things may be better than I anticipated.

A few weeks after the move, my mother took me to enroll in school at Sherrills Ford Elementary. We walked into the office, and my mother told the secretary we were there for our enrollment. A door opened, and a short chubby bald man walked out, extending his hand to my mother and saying, "Hello, I'm James Rines, the principal here at Sherrills Ford."

My mother shook his hand and said, "I'm glad to meet you."

Mr. Rines didn't have a southern accent, so I figured he was from somewhere other than North Carolina. Someone told me he was from Pennsylvania, but I wonder if that was true. Even though Mr. Rines wasn't from the south, he still insisted on every student adhering to the old southern etiquette of saying "Yes sir" and "No sir."

Being from New York, I was not used to this form of etiquette; therefore, I had trouble addressing Mr. Rines in that manner. Don't get me wrong, we were not raised to be rude children; we did say "yes" and "no," and we *never* addressed an adult by their first name. There was always a title in front of it. For example, an uncle, aunt, cousin, and Mr. or Mrs. would always precede someone considered an adult.

So, whenever Mr. Rines would ask me a question that required a yes, I wouldn't add sir to it. He would ask, "Yes, what?" And I would answer "Yes," and this would go on back and forth for a few minutes until I would finally answer, "Yes, sir"!

I suppose my views regarding this 'sir' thing was learned from my father's sister, Aunt Peggy. I told her about Mr. Rines and his demand that I call him sir. Aunt Peggy's eyes opened wide as if she had seen a ghost, and she said, "You don't have to call him sir!"

You see, Aunt Peggy, my father, and the rest of her siblings were born and raised in the segregated south. She, along with all the other black people, had no choice but to call a white man sir or suffer dire consequences for not doing so. Therefore, I suppose the pain of those times and experiences made it hard for her to envision me calling a white man sir.

I remember Aunt Peggy and I went to the mountains in Maggie Valley, North Carolina. I used to go there with her and her husband, my Uncle Bob. He was a Methodist minister, and every year the couple would go to the mountains for the United Methodist annual conference. One day Aunt Peggy and I were shopping for souvenirs at one of the local stores; as I walked around the store, my eyes went directly to a hat with a rebel flag.

At that age and time, I didn't know what a rebel flag was or its history. I just liked the colors. I picked up the hat, turned to Aunt Peggy, and said, "I want this hat."

Immediately, Aunt Peggy said, "Put it down! And find something else!"

I asked her why, then told her I liked it. She snatched the hat out of my hand, put it back on the table, and said sternly, "Pick something else!"

She slowly looked around the store to see if anyone was listening or watching us. I picked up another souvenir, paid for it, and walked back to the car. After we were in the car, Aunt Peggy explained to me what the rebel flag was and the history connected to it. You see, Aunt Peggy was an elementary school teacher who had a way of explaining things so that a young person could understand.

I started my fifth-grade year, and my first year living in North Carolina felt like I was in a nightmare. Talk about culture shock! Moving to the south in 1973 and being from the north and black was a double whammy! The white kids called me *Yankee* so often that I thought it was my name. And on those extra special days, I was called a *damn Yankee*.

A white boy name Brandon walked up to me one day and asked, "Do you know the difference between a Yankee and a damn Yankee?"

I said I didn't. Brandon said, "A Yankee comes to visit, but a damn Yankee comes to live!"

I went home that day and told my father what Brandon had said to me, and my father's response was, "Tomorrow, go to that boy and ask him if he knows what the Mason-Dixon is. Tell him that's where the Yankees go to shit, and the confederates go to eat it"

My father, like Aunt Peggy, had to endure much BS growing up. He didn't pull any punches regarding any form of discrimination. The next day, I told Brandon what my father had said, and I almost punched my ticket to see Mr. Rines!

Brandon became angry and said he would tell the teacher what I had said, but eventually, he cooled off and walked away, red-faced. The funny thing was that Brandon didn't even think about what he had been calling me because of how he was raised; only his feelings mattered to him. Eventually, I started making friends, but even they laughed and teased me about my New York accent.

Even though I had made friends, the rest of that year continued to be a challenge. I continually got into trouble which meant my mother would have to go to school and talk to Mr. Rines.

It was Christmas of 1973, the last school day before the Christmas break. I was in the art classroom, playing with clay. The bell rang, which told us school was over until after New Year. One student had thrown a ball of clay at the wall, setting off a frenzy of students throwing clay. I picked up a nice soft piece and launched it toward the wall. I thought to myself, *Wow! That felt good!* So I picked up another piece and threw it as hard as possible at the wall. This time, the clay drifted high and went through the middle of the announcement speaker at the top corner of the wall. Everyone, including myself, stopped and stared at the damaged speaker. I laughed and ran out of the room to my bus.

After we returned to school from our Christmas break, I had forgotten all about the speaker. I was in a good mood as I sat at my desk. Mr. Lofton, my homeroom teacher, walked up to me and said, "You need to go to the office and see Mr. Rines."

My good mood turned into concern. *What did I do now?* I thought. I arrived at the office where Mr. Rines was waiting. "Come on in and sit down," he said. Glaring at me, he began to say, "I understand that you were throwing clay in the art room."

I looked at him because it was apparent someone had ratted on me, and I knew my goose was cooked. '"What do you have to say about this?" asked Mr. Rines.

"I wasn't the only one throwing clay," I said.

"Well, your name was the only one I received," said Mr. Rines. "Unless you have some names you want to give?" he inquired.

"No, I don't," I replied.

Mr. Rines said, "Well, that speaker cost money; therefore, we will have to call your mother about this" Now he finally had my undivided attention. I knew I was in trouble, so I prepared mentally for the lecture (and possible butt-whipping) I figured I would get.

Two days later, my mother came in to see Mr. Rines, and he told her what had happened. Mr. Rines also said to her that they would not charge for the speaker. I think that's what saved me from the butt-whipping! My mother looked at me and said in front of Mr. Rines, "If I have to come down here again, I'm gonna half kill you!" Back then, parents could get away with a threat like that. And by the way, my mother said it; I knew she meant it! I did my best to lay low for the rest of that school year.

Time moved on, and things got better after I started the 6th grade. It was 1974, and I was beginning to get used to the slow pace of North Carolina. My main friends were Tony Herbert, Calvin Jones, and Raymond Petty. We had many things in common; therefore, it took us only a short time to become friends. The guys and I were like four peas in a pod. Tony was shy and very soft-spoken, and I never really saw him get mad. Sometimes he would get a little annoyed at people or situations, but that was rare. Tony used to hold his fork in one hand and spoon in his other simultaneously, which reminded me of a caveman. For some reason, that annoyed me. Tony loved WCW (World Championship Wrestling), and so did Calvin, Raymond, and myself. We would make Championship belts and wrestle in the boy's restroom to see who the champ was.

Calvin was quiet, but he was more outgoing than Tony. Calvin had a thin build with skinny legs; whenever he wore shorts, I would ask him if he was riding a chicken. Even though he was thin, he never backed down from a challenge. Calvin was always down for anything the group wanted to do, whether it abided by the rules or not. He was always loyal to his friends and treated people respectfully.

Raymond was a good guy. I wouldn't consider him quiet, but at the same time, he wasn't outspoken. Raymond wouldn't start a fight, but he would defend himself if backed into a corner. Raymond never liked being the butt of a joke or—as they say in the South—"being picked on." I came up with a nickname for him. I called him "Chief" because his forehead reminded me of an Indian arrow. He didn't like being called Chief, but the nickname stuck! The guys and I would taunt him by calling him Chief, putting our hands to our mouths, and then making the Indian call-*Woo! Woo! Woo!* To add to the teasing, we would dance around in a circle. It would drive him nuts, and he would try to punch us in the arms to make us stop.

I, meanwhile, was the most boastful and daring of the group. My New York roots made me feel invincible, and I didn't mind fighting either. But I knew when and how to pick my battles. At that time, I was slim and about average height for a twelve-year-old. Being from New York, I was a step or two ahead of everyone in the sixth grade (at least in my mind). I could look at a situation or problem and find the best way to benefit personally or financially.

I always thought outside the box, and many students at the school saw me as a city slicker—and to tell the truth, I felt like I was.

Chapter Two - The Business Idea

It was September of 1974, and my 6th-grade year was in full swing. It was also the start of football season. The games were usually on Fridays and would alternate between home and away.

Every Monday after a game, the bookstore would sell candy. Some of it was candy left over from the concession stand at the previous Friday night game. By the end of the month, they started selling candy every day. The guys and I would stand at a distance and watch all the kids with money—mostly white—buy candy. In 1974 you didn't have many 12-year-old black kids with extra cash to buy candy. Therefore, all we could do was sit back and salivate over those big, delicious candy bars.

There had to be a way to get some money to join in on that candy heaven. One day, we were standing at the bookstore with our mouths drooling at the candy. I noticed that the kids without money were asking their friends with money to lend them enough to buy a candy bar. Sometimes they would lend them the money, but most of the time, they would have an excuse for why they couldn't.

Just then, an idea hit me! What if my buddies and I could lend money to these kids and charge interest like a bank? We could make enough money to buy all the candy we wanted. I ran the idea through my head the whole day, trying to figure out the details, such as the rules and how the bank would operate. After sleeping on it, I thought my idea had enough detail to present to the guys.

That morning I met with the guys and presented my idea to them. Tony said, "That's a good idea, but where will we get the money to start this bank?"

"We're gonna have to scrape it together somehow," I said. We all vowed to come up with thirty-five cents each to start the bank with $1.40. I picked up soda bottles from the side of the road and took them to the store to collect the deposit. I also sold some of my precious comic books to get money.

I don't know where the other guys got their share, but everyone had their thirty-five cents to put in the following Monday. We had a meeting and planned how the bank operations would work. We would lend money out, charging a penny a day interest, and the interest started the same day you borrowed it. Interest would be charged on the day the loan was paid back. In other words, if someone took out a loan on Monday and paid it on Friday, they would owe five cents interest. The loans were capped at thirty cents, meaning if you borrowed forty cents, you would have to take out two loans, one for thirty cents and one for ten cents. Each loan would cost you a penny a day of interest. Since the banking idea was my vision, I had most of the input regarding the rules of the bank's operation and the collection of loans.

We created a loan application with a space to add the borrower's name, a space for the amount borrowed, the interest rate, a space for the borrower to sign, and a space that included the interest paid when the money was repaid. The application also had the president's signature. Since the bank was my idea, the guys decided I would be president. Accepting the role of president was one of my many mistakes. As president, my primary function was to make significant decisions concerning the bank's day-to-day operations. Other aspects of the president's job were to approve all loans that came into the bank, sign the applications, and keep the loan receipts. On some occasions, I would solicit loans. Let me add that I was also part of the muscle that helped retrieve the money from the delinquent loans.

We decided not to loan money to anyone we thought we couldn't beat. Therefore, big tough guys were not our target customers. I almost forgot a significant part of my job: Keep an eye on the money! Calvin was elected treasurer, and his job was to hold the money, keep up with the daily transactions and give us a weekly report on the balance we had in the bank. Calvin was also responsible for soliciting loans. Tony was responsible for generating loans, writing applications, and sometimes helping with loan collection; he was also responsible for watching Calvin and the money. Raymond's function was to solicit loans, help me make decisions (sort of like a vice president), help me collect outstanding loans—and to watch Calvin and our money! As you can see, all eyes were on the money. We never could agree on a name for the bank, so we just called it "The Bank."

Since there were four of us, we decided that all disputes ending in a 2 -2 tie were to be settled by flipping a coin. Thank God that never happened because that coin flip could have had disastrous results.

Chapter Three -The Hustle - The Game

It was Monday, and we were open for business! The bank had a dollar and forty cents to lend, and we were itching to get the money into the hands of our classmates. The guys and I stood there watching the bookstore from a distance waiting for our prey; eventually, Calvin, Raymond, and Tony began walking up to the kids and soliciting the loans. The tremendous response we had in lending money that day overjoyed me. On our first day, we lent out $1.35! The bank successfully financed nine loans at 15 cents each. Fifteen cents reflected the average price of a candy bar, which was 15 cents apiece. What a rush we felt after that first day.

On that Friday, the profits began to come in. We found that most loans were repaid on Fridays; therefore, we made plans for the coming Monday.

The bank had made forty-five cents profit, and it now had $1.80 to lend. That Monday, we lent out 12 fifteen-cent loans, and by Friday, we made a whopping sixty-cent profit. The bank was now worth $2.40, and we were rolling in dough! All the guys wanted to buy candy, but I convinced them to wait a week. We decided to lend money every school day to expand our customer base. Many kids needed money to buy paper, pencils, and other supplies, and who were we to deny them the chance to borrow money to get what they needed?

By the end of the third week, the bank was worth $3.20. The guys became frustrated when I suggested we wait a little longer before buying candy. Calvin asked, "I thought we started this bank to buy candy every week?"

"Yeah, that's right," said Tony. Raymond didn't say much, but I could see in his eyes that he agreed with Calvin and Tony.

I sighed and said, "Look, you all, I know what the plan for the bank was, but we can have it all if we are patient. The more money we save, the more we can lend out, which means we make a lot more profit. Besides," I said, "the candy isn't going anywhere; we'll be eating well in a few weeks."

The guys agreed begrudgingly, and we went out to lend more money. By the middle of October, the profits were so good that we finally took sixty cents from the bank to buy candy. Oh, how sweet that candy was. Every bite was pure ecstasy! The candy was a great reward and a reminder of what can happen if you work together for a common goal. By the end of October, the bank was worth $11.25, and I was approving and signing loans every day. The profits were rolling in so fast that it was like taking candy from a baby. I was shocked that so many kids needed to borrow money.

Although I knew my idea had been a good one and would bring us a little extra cash, I'd expected nothing like this. I realized that we had tapped into something far beyond our wildest dreams. Suddenly, we began to have a little swag to our walk.

We would walk the halls of the school wearing our imitation Foster Grant shades, the ones you could get at the dime store for a dime. The other students would wave at us or say hello as we walked. It was like we were movie stars—but deep down, I knew we were getting too much attention, and if the teachers discovered what we were doing, it would be the bank's end, and we'd be in serious trouble.

One day, I called an emergency meeting and told the guys, "Look, we are drawing too much attention to ourselves. We have got to find a way to be less noticeable. And we need to stay away from Frankie Jones." Frankie Jones was a seventh grader, a bully with size, strength, and sadistic tendencies who particularly enjoyed inflicting pain on others smaller than himself. Another quirk of his was that he was an instigator who took great pleasure in starting fights between kids.

Tagging along Frankie was his sidekick, a kid named Roger Hanson, who would help him torment others. Roger was also reasonably big, though not quite the bully Frankie was—at least not yet. However, he still inflicted his fair share of pain and torment on others. Even though Frankie and Roger were black, they both were equally opportunistic bullies.

The number one rule of the bank was never to lend money to Frankie and Roger and, *for God's sake*, never let them find out about what we were doing. Rule number two was never to lend any money to anyone we felt we couldn't beat. There were occasions when Raymond and I had to get rough with guys who didn't want to pay their loans back. There was a guy named Jerry Rice. Jerry had borrowed thirty cents and refused to pay it back. Jerry's payback total was fifty cents when you added in the interest. He said he had no money when we asked him about the money.

One day Raymond and I saw Jerry out on the field during PE. We walked up to him, and I asked, "Where's the money?"

He grinned at us and answered, "I'm not paying you anything!"

Raymond and I looked at each other in disbelief. Before I could speak, Raymond punched Jerry in the stomach. Jerry bent over in obvious pain, and I asked him again, "Where's the money?"

Jerry looked at me from his bent-over position and spat, "Go to Hell!"

This time I threw an uppercut punch which hit him in the chest, causing him to stand upright again. And I followed that punch with another blow to his chest, which caused him to fall to the ground. Raymond and I went through Jerry's pockets and retrieved fifty cents. He had more than fifty cents on him, but the way I saw it, we weren't thieves. We were businessmen, and so we only took what money was owed to us.

Now and then, the guys we thought to be pushovers were more formidable than they looked. On the other hand, the girls that borrowed money were usually faithful to paying back their loans. When they didn't, we would give them a pass. We didn't want to be known for roughing up girls! The bank wouldn't lend to them again. Things were going well, and the money we made was almost unheard of for black youth in 1974. I was still surprised by the success of the bank. And I never expected the level of growth and success that we were having at that point. But, as luck would have it, things would take a slight turn for the worse.

Every school has students whose elevators don't go to the top floor. Our almost-top-floor guy was Tony Holliday. Tony was a seventh-grade white dude with what we used to call *crazy eyes* or *cock eyes*. One eye looked to the left, the other slightly up and to the right. It amazed me how he never walked into a wall. I often wondered how he was in the same school as the rest of us because you had to listen closely to him to understand what he was saying. Sometimes I thought he was speaking another language.

Don't get me wrong, I never made fun of him, and I'm not doing it now, but the truth's the truth. Tony was as strong as an ox and would do anything people told or asked him to do. I remember that Frankie and Roger would get Tony to do crazy things to people. Sometimes I felt that Frankie and Roger were onto what the guys and I were doing. They seemed to be constantly watching us closely.

One day, I was coming out of my classroom, and Frankie yelled at Tony and said, "Hey Tony, Aldric is laughing at your pants!" Tony's pants were always what we used to call high waters. But I had never commented on them and hadn't said a word about them when Frankie began instigating this particular situation. Tony walked up to me and asked, "You laughing at my pants?"

I could barely understand what he was saying with the drool running down his chin. For a second, I wasn't even sure he was talking to me the way his crazy eyes were looking in different directions. I told Tony I didn't say a thing about his pants, and I tried to walk away. As I started to walk around him, he knocked my books out of my hand. When I bent over to pick up my books, the crazy fool bent down and grabbed me.

The next thing I knew, I was upside down with my legs in the air and my head facing the floor! Tony would pick me up and continuously slam my lower half down. I tried my best to throw uppercut punches to his midsection. Whenever he picked me up and slammed me to the floor, my legs would slide as if I were sliding on ice. Pain shot through my body as my knees hit the floor. Since he had my arms pinned, throwing punches was hard, but I did my best. I guess Tony got tired of seeing my butt in his face as he continuously lifted me, so he let me go. As I looked around, I noticed that a big crowd had gathered to see the action. I could only thank God that there wasn't a teacher anywhere in the vicinity. The guys and I were supposed to remain low-key and not bring any attention to our group. The incident was most definitely an attention grabber.

Not only did I lose some self-esteem, but I also lost the respect of some of our customers. Frankie and Roger got a good laugh from what they had just instigated. I walked around, embarrassed and confused about what had just happened to me. There was a girl in my class named Candy, and she was a good friend of mine. I sometimes wonder if our relationship was more than friends. At that time, I was busy with the bank—I didn't have time for girls. At least, that's what I thought. She walked up from behind me, put her arm around my neck, and said, "Don't worry, Aldric, Tony didn't beat you. You won that fight." Candy would eventually learn about the bank, but since I think she had a little crush on me, I was confident she wouldn't tell. She became a good customer.

After the Tony incident, I knew we had to be more forceful in collecting late payments. That would restore my respect and confidence. We were walking a thin tightrope. Raymond and I wouldn't hesitate to rough someone up that wouldn't pay. As the money continued to roll in, we became increasingly paranoid that the school staff would discover the bank. By the middle of November, the bank was worth $14.85. We decided to buy some candy to reward ourselves for our hard work. I couldn't wrap my mind around the fact that we hadn't been caught operating the bank. We were writing many loans and using scare tactics to collect the money. Lady Luck was on our side—but Lady Luck could be a fickle thing at times. I found out that she could pack her bags and leave you anytime!

Mr. Lofton was our 6th-grade homeroom teacher, and he was also our math and science teacher. The 6th grade was the first time we changed classes since I began school. We would have Mr. Lofton for part of the day and Miss Lafone for the rest.

Mr. Lofton was a medium-sized thin guy who, to me, acted a little feminine or, as some would say, "a little soft." Looking back, he reminded me of John Ritter, who played in the television show *Three's Company*. Mr. Lofton was a busybody, always sticking his nose where I thought it didn't belong. He would walk up from behind, look over your shoulder and try to see what you were doing. Mr. Lofton knew I was up to something, but he couldn't figure out what it was. I could look into his eyes and see how badly he wanted to catch me doing something wrong.

The guys and I tried our best to stay under the radar, but as I'd suspected earlier, Lady Luck had packed her bags and was about to go on vacation! In our class, there was a white boy named Scott Mackey. Scott was a short, rough-looking little guy. He came from a low-income family, and his clothes looked like they hadn't been washed in weeks, nor did his body. Don't get me wrong; I'm not putting Scott down because my family was not the Rockefellers either. But white kids like Scott still thought they were better than black people because that's what they had been taught.

One day, while in Mr. Lofton's class, Scott and my desks were beside each other. One of our classmates was a big girl named Beverly, and Beverly had an enormous chest. Scott and I were making jokes about Beverly and her massive boobs. I told Scott, "I can see your head disappear between her big boobs!"

Everyone in the class started laughing, and it seemed to rub Scott wrong. So, Scott decided to throw a pencil at me. The pencil hit me in my chest. I picked it up and threw it back at him. Scott responded by calling me a black son of a bitch! I lost it and jumped up from my desk and grabbed him. I punched him in the head a few times. Then I grabbed his hair from the back and began bouncing his head off the deck top. Just then, Mr. Lofton ran towards us and broke up the fight. He grabbed both of us by the arm and walked us up to Mr. Rines's office.

When we arrived at the secretary's desk, Mr. Rines stepped out of his office and asked, "What's going on here?"

Mr. Lofton answered, saying, "These two boys were fighting."

I yelled out, "He called me a black son of a bitch!"

The office secretary, whom I remember had those black horn-rimmed glasses, gasped in shock and covered her mouth. Mr. Rines said, "Ok, you boys go into my office."

Mr. Rines walked into his office and pulled his keys from his pocket. "So, you boys were fighting?" he asked. I thought it was a crazy question because Mr. Lofton had already told him it was the reason for our visit. Of course, I didn't let him know my thoughts about his question. He walked to a tall metal locker, opened it, and pulled out a paddle. Back then, corporal punishment was accepted and encouraged. The paddles were usually made of wood, but this one was made of fiberglass and had holes drilled. The holes made the paddle more aerodynamic to cut down on the drag from the wind as it swung forward—and the holes also helped increase the pain.

Usually, when students were getting paddled, there was supposed to be a second adult to be a witness. Mr. Rines ordered Scott to bend over, and Scott complied. The next thing I heard was a sharp whack.

Whack! Whack! Whack!

Scott began to cry uncontrollably, shaking as his face grew beet red. Mr. Rines asked Scott, "Are you going to fight anymore?"

Scott replied, "No, Sir!"

"Are you going to call people names?"

"No, Sir!"

I must admit that I took a little pleasure watching the guy who just called me a black S.O.B. getting his behind whooped. But then the reality hit me—my whooping was next, and the little smirk I had slid slowly off my face.

As Scott was standing there shaking with tears rolling down his red face, Mr. Rines told him to return to his classroom. I stood with my arms folded as I watched Scott walk out the door, looking like he had been put in a blender. I bent forward while putting my hands on Mr. Rines's desk. I was ready to take the paddle like a man even though I was shaking inside like an old washing machine on a spin cycle. Just then, Mr. Rines sat on his desk and put his paddle down. He said, "Sit down, Aldric. I want to talk to you."

I had a look of shock on my face. I thought that I was a victim of some joke. I slowly eased myself down and sat on the desk beside Mr. Rines, who looked at me and said, "Aldric, unfortunately, we live in a time where people are going to call you names that you don't like. I'm sorry about this, but that's how it is. Just because someone calls you a name you don't like doesn't mean you have to use violence. I'm trying to tell you, Aldric, that you will have to control your temper. Do you understand, young man?"

I said, "Yes, I understand."

I was shocked that he didn't paddle me but instead gave me such an emotional speech. Mr. Rines told me to go back to my classroom and for me to stay out of trouble. I had many paddlings in school that I have forgotten, but I have always remembered the day I didn't get one and the words Mr. Rines said to me. As I walked out of the office, I thought Mr. Rines understood me and was on my side. But I later discovered that my newfound feelings about Mr. Rines were premature!

Walking back into the classroom, I could see and feel that all eyes were on me, expecting to see me all torn up like Scott. I smiled as I sat down at my desk. One of the kids asked me, "Didn't you get the paddle?"

I said, "No, I didn't."

Still crying, Scott looked over at me and asked, "You didn't?"

I looked at him with a little smirk and kindly said, "No." I didn't realize at the time that Scott wasn't finished with me by a long shot. This grudge he was holding would be long-lasting. As the old saying goes, "Payback is hell," especially when you're doing something against the rules.

After the confrontation with Scott, Raymond came to me and asked, "I thought you said we needed to lay low and not bring attention to ourselves?"

"Yeah, you're right," I told him, "but sometimes you must respond to things that happen. I will try to do better." That day, I promised the guys I would try my best to avoid bringing more attention to the group.

Unfortunately, that promise was short-lived.

Two days after the promise, the boys in each class were told to assemble in the hallway outside the boy's restroom. We were told that someone had taken a crap on the bathroom floor! Mr. Rines wanted every boy to go in and look. A steady stream of boys in single file walked through the restroom as if we were getting our food in the lunch line. When my turn came, I walked in and looked down at what looked like a four-inch turd! As I walked out, I thought, who would be crazy enough to take a dump on the floor? I began to laugh, imagining someone who couldn't quite make it to the toilet, and the turd fell out. Mr. Rines, standing outside the door, asked, "Aldric, did you see something funny?"

Still laughing, I looked at him and answered, "No."

Mr. Rines asked me, "No, what?"

Then we played our usual back-and-forth game until I finally said, "No, Sir!"

Mr. Rines began one of his long lectures about respect and hygiene. After the public lecture at the boy's bathroom, I was told by Mr. Lofton to go to the office, where I received an extended, up close, and personal version of the address. After my private lecture, Mr. Rines informed me that he would be watching me. Once again, I had brought attention to myself, which could bring awareness to the bank.

It was a miracle that the bank hadn't been discovered. As luck would have it, weeks later, I had another distraction that almost cost us everything. Her name was Anita Johnson. Anita was a popular girl in school, and she knew it. She was only 13 years old but had a grown woman's body. Therefore, a lot of older guys were attracted to her. She wasn't the prettiest girl I had ever seen, but her body got her into doors that other less-developed girls couldn't. She was in the sixth grade because she had failed it the year before. I hadn't hit my growth spurt, so Anita stood about an inch or two taller than me. And, of course, she was way more mature. I would see her at functions with high school guys, and although only 13 years old, Anita seemed to fit in with them.

For some reason, far beyond my understanding, Anita took a liking to me; she liked that I was from New York and was attracted to my New York accent. I wasn't bad-looking and was certainly different from the other boys she knew—but on the other hand, I had no idea how to act around her. After a few weeks with Anita, I realized I was out of her league.

Don't get me wrong; I loved the attention I would get when we were together at football games and other functions. Most of the guys would wonder how I got to be with a girl like her. My chest would stick out like a roster as we walked hand and hand down the school hallways.

I thought I was in love, but she was only in the relationship with me to play with my mind—and she was a master at it! After Anita hooked me, she would toy with me by breaking up and then making up with me. The emotional roller coaster she had me on would soon affect my relationship with the guys and the bank. I was slipping, and they knew it. I had stopped paying attention to details, and my mind drifted away from the bank business.

One day Calvin approached me and said, "We have to talk." I asked him what we needed to talk about, and he said, "The bank."

So, I walked with him outside, where Tony and Raymond were waiting. "What's the problem?" I asked.

"The problem is you are not focused on the bank, and it's hurting all of us," said Raymond. I stared into space like I was in some trance.

Calvin said, "You are letting your love life mess up all our money!" Something inside me snapped, and I lunged for Calvin. I grabbed him by the front of his shirt and tried to pull him towards me. Tony and Raymond jumped in between Calvin and me to stop the scuffle.

"Stop it!" yelled Raymond as he pushed us apart.

Calvin yelled obscenities at me, and I lunged for him again. This time Tony put me in a bear hug while yelling for me to stop it. The bank was in jeopardy, and we all knew it.

Finally, I walked away and started back to the classroom. My mind was reeling, and I could visualize my great idea crumbling right before my eyes. I had to figure out what I would do to stop this downward chain of events. By the next day, I had calmed down and began to think more clearly. I thought about everything we had done to make this bank work, and I didn't want to lose it like this. Therefore, when I got to school, I went to Calvin and apologized to him for grabbing him. The two of us talked about what had happened and shook hands. I realized that I needed to think deeply about the relationship between Anita and myself.

That week Anita broke up with me for the tenth time, and I finally decided I'd had enough. I resolved not to pursue her anymore. My efforts to convince her to stay with me were hurting both me and my business. Reality hit me hard, and I finally accepted that I wasn't in her league. Therefore, I moved on from her. After the final break up, whenever I would pass Anita in the hallways, she would cut her eyes at me with a big smirk. As time passed, I began to pay more attention to the details of the bank and less attention to Anita.

By the end of November, the bank was worth $20.00, and the loan applications were coming in so good that we bought ourselves some candy. It was December, and Christmas was coming. We knew that loans would be going out fast and furious, and I was beginning to worry that we may not have enough money in the bank to meet the demand. Christmas came and went without incident, and thankfully we had enough money to cover the market. January 1975 came in with a bang, and the bank was worth $28.00.

The bank was a little slow during the first two weeks of the month because all the students had the after-Christmas blues. But by the end of January, things had picked up again with the bank, and all the students were back in full swing, borrowing money again. I was busy approving loans or collecting late payments.

I remember a teacher once told me that you should never make the person you're going to fight afraid of you because a scared person will do any and everything they can to get you off of them. A student named Jimmy Collins was the first person to show me the truth behind that philosophy. Jimmy was a short, slim white boy who was somewhat sheepish and looked tailor-made for a bully. Jimmy had borrowed fifteen cents and had yet to pay back the money. Threatening him didn't work, so I resorted to playing hardball. Little did I know that the threats had indeed made Jimmy afraid.

The guys and I were hanging out in the hallway one day when Calvin spotted Jimmy coming toward us. I looked around to see if anyone else was in the hallway. There were no witnesses to be found. I thought, *This is the right time to implement our zero-tolerance policy.* Calvin, who always kept the unpaid loans in his notebook, pulled Jimmy's application out and handed it to me.

As Jimmy walked by, I grabbed him by his arm and pulled him into a hallway closet. I turned the light on while closing the door. ``Where's the money?" I asked. Jimmy responded by saying, "I don't have it." I responded by punching him in the stomach. The next few minutes were a blur! Jimmy lit into me like a wild man fighting for his life. I couldn't get a punch in to save my life! We bounced off the walls as if we were at a punk rock concert. Jimmy got tired of hitting me, so he stopped, opened the closet door, and walked out. I walked out a few seconds later, looking like I had been put in a blender. Calvin and Tony looked at me in shock. I walked past them and tore Jimmy's loan note without saying a word.

The fight, if that's what you want to call it, with Jimmy reminded me of another time I picked on the wrong guy. There was an Italian boy in New York named Philip Lansalatti. Phillip was one of my best friends, and we always hung out in school; he was a short skinny little guy who constantly chewed nervously on his fingernails. Phillip looked like it would only take one punch to knock him out. He was more of a follower than a leader. One day we got into an argument. I don't even remember what the disagreement was about, but I do remember it was intense.

Out of the blue, I decided to give Phillip a slap across his face. Phillip jumped on me like a caged raccoon. I was thanking God that some other kids broke it up. I walked away with snot, blood from my nose, and scratches all over my face and body. I should have learned right then never to judge a book by its cover. The guys and I never talked about the day I decided to take Jimmy into the closet, nor did we ever lend Jimmy any more money.

It was the end of January, and the bank was worth $33! The guys looked forward to the end of the school year because we decided that the money would be divided among the four of us. We all loved making money because, in our eyes, money meant power, and money and power got the girls' attention.

But we also understood that girls might bring more attention to the bank than we wanted. (Anita was a big lesson for us all.) Don't get me wrong, many girls knew what we were doing, but only a few that we trusted knew the bank's inner workings. And only one or two knew the amount of money we were making. As time passed, we were amazed that we hadn't been caught yet. Mr. Lofton was watching us like a hawk. He knew we were up to something, but he just couldn't put his finger on it. It was like a game of cat and mouse. He stared at me; I felt he wanted me worse than Calvin, Tony, and Raymond. Mr. Lofton would slowly walk past my desk, scanning it as if he was looking for something. I would look up at him and give him a bright smile as he frowned, turning his head and walking away.

It was the middle of February, and things were going well with the bank. We never thought we could make this much money running an under-the-radar bank. We felt like nothing could stop us now. I thought to myself, we're going to skate through the rest of the year with no more problems. Boy, oh Boy, was I wrong. Along came Big John!

John Danner was his name, and he was so large that everyone would call him Big John. Most people would call him the gentle giant because he was soft-spoken and friendly. Big John towered over most of the kids at the school as if they were dwarfs, and the guys and I were no exception. He was at least 250 pounds and stood about five foot nine inches. That's huge for a sixth-grader. Big John was so big that he had problems with his foot arches which caused him to take baby steps and walk with a wobble. Even Though Big John was considered a gentle giant, he had a temper, especially when he was teased or confronted incorrectly. Once a fellow sixth-grader named Ray McCleave thought it would be a good idea to tease big John about how he walked. Ray was a pretty big guy, and was also what we called an instigator and troublemaker.

Big John turned and grabbed Ray, picked him up, and slammed him against the wall like a rag doll. It took several teachers to make Big John let go of Ray. I knew from that day that Big John had a terrible temper if provoked. One day Tony brought me a loan application from Big John for thirty cents. Tony took the application, knowing we had a rule against lending to big guys. Deep down, I knew I shouldn't sign the approval of the loan but against my better judgment, I signed it. I thought, hey, John's a friendly, easy-going guy; therefore, we shouldn't have a problem with him. I had done some knuckle-headed things in the past, but signing that loan, I realized later, would take the cake.

Two weeks passed, and Raymond told me Big John still needed to pay his loan. Although we have yet to establish a time frame for the loan to be paid back, we still expect it to be paid promptly. Because even though we made a lot more money the longer the loan was out, we realized that after about a week, it was harder to collect our money. The interest would get high after a week or two, and so we also discovered that sometimes the borrower could not pay all the money.

I called a meeting with the guys and asked them what they thought we should do about big John not paying the loan yet. Calvin said, "You approved the loan, so you deal with it."

I shrugged my shoulders and said, "Yeah, I know I did it, but pointing fingers won't get our money back."

We all agreed that the group approach would be best and that we would wait until the right time and place to ask big John for the money.

Later that day, I saw big John walking down the hallway, so I ran and gathered the guys, and we followed him as he walked into the restroom. Big John was standing in front of the urinal, so we stood by the sink waiting for him to finish. Big John turned toward us with a puzzled look on his face.

"What are you looking at?" he asked.

Since I was president and approved the loan, it was my place to answer. I stepped forward, and with a slight tremble in my voice, I asked," John do you remember that we lent you thirty cents two weeks ago?"

"Yeah, what about it?" John asked.

I said, "Well, we were wondering if you would pay it back?"

John answered, "I don't have any money right now, so I will pay when I get it." I looked back at the guys to reassure myself that I had some backup. But the guys had a cut-and-run look on their faces. I thought to myself, *I'm from New York!* And I thought about a poem I had heard when I lived there.

We are the boys from the ville,

We never run and never will.

We throw down till we go down!

I looked at big John and responded, "Look, you borrowed the money, so now you need to pay it back!"

Big John just stood there like he was in some trance.

Since he didn't say anything, I began to get bolder and put a little bass in my voice. I said, "You owe us thirty cents plus interest, big boy!"

Big John's eyes opened wide, and he grunted as he grabbed and picked me up in a bear hug. My feet dangled off the floor as John squeezed me like an anaconda. His breath smelled like spoiled milk, and I detected some bad B.O.!

I looked over at the guys, who looked as if they were in shock. I yelled, "Help me!"

Raymond jumped on big John's back and put him in a chokehold. Calvin and Tony dived to the floor and grabbed big John around his legs. Big John spun around so fast that Calvin slid across the floor as Tony hung on for dear life! Big John fell into one of the bathroom stalls and slammed Raymond, who was still on his back, banging him against the wall above the toilet. Raymond flies off, landing beside the commode while I'm still being hugged and going for the ride. Tony was still trying to hang on while being dragged on the floor like a mop.

At this point, I didn't know where Calvin was. As big John went forward out of the stall, I began to slip from his grip. At the same time, Tony pulled one of his legs out from under him, and he fell forward, slamming my back against the sink and hitting his forehead on the mirror above the sink, cracking it. I fell to the floor in pain as big John staggered back like Frankenstein and fell to the floor, almost unconscious—but not quite. His eyes were flickering, and he was still breathing. Believe it or not, we didn't see any blood.

Calvin finally appeared in my sight as I got up from the floor. Raymond and Tony were both on their feet, so we walked over and looked down on big John. John was groaning while he moved his head back and forth. We looked at each other in silence, not knowing what to do. Since John wasn't dead, we all decided to run out of the boy's restroom and tell no one what had just happened.

But before I left, I searched big John's pockets for money since he was down and almost out. I didn't find any money—only a piece of gum that I took for my troubles, Then I ran out of the boy's restroom.

The rest of that day, we didn't see big John, and we didn't hear about what happened. The next day all the boys in each class were summoned to the boy's restroom by Mr. Rines for a tour and to see the cracked mirror. After a ten-minute lecture about destroying school property, Mr. Rines told us to return to our classroom. As I walked by Mr. Rines, he looked down at me with an I'm watching you look. Deep down, I think he knew I had something to do with the broken mirror, but he had no proof.

Calvin and I stopped to watch all the boys return to their classrooms. That's when I saw him! Big John was walking towards us. He walked as if he were walking in the mud because of his arches, and as he got closer to us, I could see a pretty big knot on his forehead. My heart pounded in fear, and My legs became weak. I wanted to run, but I couldn't move. Calvin looked at me with fear in his eyes. He was also petrified and couldn't run. When Big John finally reached us, my mind could only think about the severe beating Calvin and I was about to get.

Big John's arm extended as if he were trying to give me something. Yes! He had something in his hand. I reached out my hand, and big John dropped thirty cents in it. And without saying a word, he turned and walked away. Calvin and I looked at each other in disbelief.

Calvin said, "What the hell?"

"I don't know," I replied.

I was very relieved that we got our money from big John and we didn't get a beating, but I did notice that he didn't pay the interest on the loan. But after further thought, I felt it was best to leave that alone. Therefore we moved on with the promise that we would never loan money to big John again.

(P.S: Big John never said a word to anyone about what happened in the restroom, and Mr. Rines never found out who broke the mirror.)

***

Once again, we had dodged a bullet, and we might have smooth sailing from now on. It was now the end of February, and the bank was worth $40.00. For some reason, Frankie had a problem with me. I never did anything to him, but he acted as I had. The fact that I was from New York bothered him somehow. I got the feeling that he was a tad jealous of me because of my northern accent and the attention I received from it, good or bad.

One day Frankie walked up to the guys and me. He looked at me and said, "I know you boys are up to something because I heard some things."

"What did you hear?" I asked.

"Don't worry about what I heard!" he responded. Frankie stepped towards me, looked me in the eye, and said, "I know you guys are lending money to people."

I looked at the guys, then looked back at Frankie and said, "We're not lending money. I just lent a few friends money so they could buy candy."

"Yeah, right," said Frankie. I looked around for Roger because the two were always together. Sure enough, a few seconds later, Roger came around the corner.

"What are these little gourd-head boys up to now?" he asked. Ironically, that summer, Roger and I became good friends. He lived just up the road from me, and I spent the night over at his house many times; we remained friends for many years after that summer.

"These little punks are trying to tell me they aren't lending money," Frankie answered.

"We're not," Calvin said.

"Who pulled your chain, you little punk?" asked Roger. Just then, Mr. Walker, the English teacher, walked past us and entered his classroom. That was the sign for Frankie and Roger to split the scene. As Frankie walked past me, he raised his hand as if he would give me a Jap Slap.

Back in the day, we used to walk up to someone seriously or play and swing our right or left arm back like we were going to backhand them. Then we would lean forward, lifting our body with one foot on its tiptoe and the other leg swinging towards the back. That's the definition of a Jap Slap! I put my hands up in defense as Frankie drew his hand back.

Frankie said, "Yeah, that's right, put up those hands! That's what I want!"

I knew he wanted that, but I figured he would kill me if I did. And I also knew when to hold them and when to fold them. Plus, I wanted to avoid bringing more attention to the bank.

We had to be especially careful now that Frankie and Roger were on to what we were doing. The pressure was on because not only did we have Mr. Lofton watching us, but we now also had to deal with these two knuckleheads.

In the sixth grade, we had to change classes, so a large part of our day we spent in Mr. Lofton's class, and the second half of the day was spent with Miss. Lafone. Miss Lafone was a southern woman with a heavy southern accent. Since I wasn't used to her southern twang, it took work to understand her sometimes. Miss Lafone was an overweight redhead that had a bad temper at times. Nonetheless, she seemed to like me for some reason, and she would tell me that she loved my northern accent. She was sometimes tough to read, and I could never understand her hot and cold moods or attitude. Some days it seemed like she loved me, and others seemed like she wanted to paddle my butt off!

Miss Lafone once asked me if I wanted to spend my summer vacation with her and had the nerve to ask me to ask my mom and dad if I could do it! I didn't know what her intentions were, and at my age, I didn't understand. The guys and I were running a pretty profitable bank under her nose, but she was beginning to watch us closer and closer. I began to feel the pressure from the day-to-day grind of running the bank under the radar, but the money was too good to stop. It was like the money was a drug; the more we made, the more we wanted.

As the pressure mounted, I began to let things distract me and began slipping again. The bank was doing great regarding sales, but the guys and I were getting paranoid. Paranoia leads to mistrust, and that leads to distrust, and that leads to bad blood. Tony was questioning the money handling, and Calvin was angry that Tony was questioning the cash handling. Raymond was upset with me because I always brought unwanted attention to the bank. And I was getting sick of all of them. The bank was starting to crumble again. I had to do something before we lost everything.

I called a meeting to air our grievances and find a way to move forward. Everyone had their say, and then I told the guys, "We have come so far, and we were making too much money to let the bank end like this. I told them that even though the bank was my idea, we all owned it.

March was an excellent month, and by the end of it, the bank was worth $49.00. On the first of April, we decided not to spend any money from the profits to have more to divide at the end of the school year. The pressure was still on, but I tried not to let it get to me. By now, Mr. Lofton, Miss Lafone, Frankie, and Roger were watching our every move. A clown in a circus couldn't juggle everything we were doing to cover up the bank.

Even though we worked hard not to bring attention to the bank, a dark cloud always seemed to follow us. By mid-April, the bank was worth $54, which was more money than we had ever had in our young life. Considering the minimum wage in 1975 was $1.60 per hour, what we had done was quite an accomplishment. Things were going well, the loans were going out, and profits were coming in. We were on top of the world. The bank was everything the guys and I had hoped it would be. Everything was running in perfect harmony. But as I had said earlier, things you do in the past can and will come back to haunt you. Little did we know that the harmony train was about to come off the rails!

One morning, I was walking down the hallway and noticed Scott and Mr. Lofton coming out of Mr. Rines's office. Something didn't look right about this picture, and I wasn't quite sure what was happening. As I got closer to Scott, he looked at me with a sinister grin. Right then, I had the feeling that I might be in deep trouble. I could feel the knife going into my back, and I whispered, "I know payback is hell."

I had lent Scott money before the bank took off, and we never lent it to him again after our fight. Scott never knew about the plans for the bank and its scope. He never filled out an application because we hadn't created them then. So as far as Scott knew, I was only lending him money. Later that day, Mr. Lofton said I needed to report to Mr. Rines's office. Scott had seen me giving someone money, and he saw someone paying me money. Therefore, Scott told Mr. Lofton that I was lending money and roughing boys up to get it back. Scott was sore at me because I didn't get paddled after our fight.

Scott added a little to the story to make me look bad and to ensure I would get the paddle this time. I walked into Mr. Rines's office; he pointed at me and said, "Sit Down!"

I sat down as Mr. Rines leaned forward, looked into my eyes, and said, "I understand that you are strong-arming students and taking their money."

"No, Sir!"

"Then are you lending boys money?"

I answered with my fingers crossed. "I lend my friends money sometimes, and they pay me back. But, I never forced or roughed up anyone for their money."

"Well," said Mr. Rines. "That's what I've been hearing from Mr. Lofton, but since I have no evidence, I guess I will let you go for now."

As I got up to walk out the door, Mr. Rines added, "I promise you one thing, mister. I will be watching you. Do you understand?"

I answered yes.

"Yes, what?"

I turned with a smile on my face. "Yes, sir!"

The next day while changing classes, I went into the boy's bathroom to take a leak. While standing at the urinal, I heard the door open, and someone walked in. I turned my head to see who had come in, and it was Frankie and Roger.

"Well, well," Frankie said. “Look who we’ve got here."

I replied, "Look, guys, I don't want any trouble."

As I turned toward them, Frankie grabbed me by my collar and said, "You gonna get some trouble. Where's the money?"

"What money?"

"You know what money we're talking about," said Roger.

"Guys, like I said before, I'm not doing anything, and I don't have any money."

The door opened, and in came Calvin, Raymond, and Tony. "Leave him alone!" said Raymond.

Frankie let me go, and he and Roger walked toward Raymond. "What the hell are you girls gonna do?" Frankie asked.

I walked over and stood with the guys. We put up our fists with a look on our faces that said we were willing to take a beat down for solidarity. As Frankie and Roger moved towards us, the door opened, and in walked Mr. Moore! Mr. Moore was one of the teachers at the school. We started walking away in different directions as if nothing was going on.

Mr. Moore looked at us. "What are you boys doing hanging out in the restroom? Why aren't you headed to class?"

"We are on our way now," I answered.

"Well, let's go," said Mr. Moore.

We exited the boy's room and walked toward our class. "I promise I will see you girls later," said Frankie.

Later that month, I did another boneheaded thing that brought attention to us. I had another friend named Tony, who gave me a pringles potato chip can full of grape gumballs. Tony's family had a gumball machine at his house, and he accidentally rolled a tire into it, breaking it. Therefore, Tony decided to bring me some. That day Mrs. Lafone had taken the whole class outside for P.E. On our way back to the classroom, I was handing out gumballs, and an old beagle dog walked up to me.

I looked down at him and decided to give him a gumball. I dropped the gumball on the ground, and the beagle licked it a few times and walked away. I picked the gumball up and was about to throw it into the woods but, just then, a guy named Steven Eades walked up.

"Give me some gum," he said.

I thought about it for a second, and then I handed him the gum that the dog had licked. Steven put the gum in his mouth, and with a big grin, he began chewing it. All the kids started laughing and told Steven that the dog had licked the gum. Steven stopped chewing, and his face turned beet red. What I didn't know at that time was that Miss. Lafone was right behind us, and she overheard the kids telling Steve that I gave him a gumball that the dog had licked!

Miss. Lafone looked at me and yelled, "Did you give Steven a gumball that the dog licked?" And before I could answer, she shouted, "Because if you did, I'm gonna paddle your behind!"

At first, I looked at the witnesses, who looked confused and afraid. I'm sure they thought I would pay them back later if they told on me—and, of course, I would have.

I looked up at Miss. Lafone said, "No, I didn't!"

She looked at the other kids and then looked at me with a frown on her fat face and said, "You better not have." I realized that I had dodged a huge bullet and huge paddling. To this day, I still don't understand why I did the self-destructive things I did. It was just youthful immaturity and a little stupidity!

Chapter Four - Game Over

The end of May was coming quickly. Since we only had a few weeks of school left, the guys and I closed the bank and divided the money among the four of us.

At the time of closing, the Bank had $60 in the account. None of us had ever had that much money at one time in our lives! We each got $15 a piece and were so excited that we could hardly contain ourselves. The money was burning our pockets, ready to spend. I destroyed all the receipts and all evidence from the bank. What a feeling it was to have money in our pockets and spend it like a big shot.

That weekend I went on a shopping spree! I bought candy, sodas, and toys. I was like a drug addict in a warehouse full of drugs. Fifteen dollars went a long way back then, and I spent it with reckless abandonment. When I came down from my spending high, I only had seventy-five cents left.

That Monday, I was back in school and feeling great. It was the last week of school, and the summer break was here.

Back in the day, the schools had this old wooden desk that had a place under the seat to place your books. I decided to clean out my desk. While sitting, I reached under the seat and tried to pull all the books out simultaneously with one hand. One of the books fell to the floor, and a stack of maybe 50 bank receipts was exposed. My eyes opened so wide you would have thought I'd seen a ghost! In a panic, I reached down to grab the papers and found myself staring at a pair of brown wingtip shoes. I looked up slowly, only to find Mr. Lofton looking down at the receipts on the floor.

Mr. Lofton bent over to pick up one of the receipts and read it. He bent down once more and picked up the rest of the receipts. He straightened the papers and slowly skimmed through them as he casually walked out of the classroom. It was so quiet in the room that you could have heard a pin drop. Then the whispering started. Since most of the class were former clients, they knew trouble was coming my way. I knew I was in trouble, and I tried to focus on what I would say to get out of this mess. I tried not to panic. I just sat there calmly, waiting for the hammer to drop as the sweat ran down my neck.

About five minutes later, Mr. Lofton returned to the classroom and stood by his desk. Then I heard Mr. Rines's animated voice calling out names as he walked through the classroom door. "John Brown! Borrowed thirty cents at a penny a day interest. Signed Aldric Fishe, president!"

Mr. Rines walked over, sat down at Mr. Lofton's desk, and began yelling out more names as he shuffled through the receipts. "Becky Gabriel! Borrowed thirty cents at a penny a day interest. Signed Aldric Fishe, president!"

"Jerry Hildebran! Borrowed thirty cents at a penny a day interest. Signed Aldric Fishe, President!"

"Candy Reid! Borrowed twenty cents at one cent a day interest, signed Aldric Fishe president!"

By now, the whole class was looking at me. Some of them were laughing, while others had a look of shock on their faces. Their shocked faces surprised me because most of them were my former customers. Maybe it was the fact that I had been caught that shocked them.

Mr. Rines stood up from the desk, walked to the chalkboard, and said, "Let us look at how much one cent a day costs the borrowers." Within ten minutes, Mr. Rines dissected the whole bank operation and made me look like the ultimate loan shark. He was telling the class and illustrating how I was ripping them off. Mr. Rines told the class that I was taking advantage of them. And then, after he finished killing me softly with his words, he said, "Mr.Fishe, Come with me." While I walked to the classroom door, I glanced over at my fellow bank partners. They all had shocked and worried looks on their faces.

As I was taking the walk of shame, I thought about what my mother and father would do to me, and my legs began to weaken. *No one can help me now*, I thought.

As Mr. Rines and I walked into his office, he told me to sit down. I sat down on a chair that was in front of his desk. Mr. Rines leaned back in his chair and asked,

"Okay, Aldric, who was in on the scam with you?" "Because I know that you didn't do this by yourself."

I looked into his stone-cold eyes and answered, "No one helped me. I ran the bank all by myself."

The unwritten rule was never to give up your friends, no matter what. Besides, we all had talked about the possibility of getting caught, and every man would go down himself. But talk is cheap when you're in the type of trouble I was in for. I felt that I should be the one to fall on the sword because the whole thing had been my idea; I was president. Like the captain of a ship, I was willing to go down with my operation.

Mr. Rines sprang forward in his seat like he was shot out of a cannon and asked, "Do you think I'm stupid enough to believe you did this by yourself?"

I answered, "As I said, I did it all alone."

"Don't lie to me, son; I know you were not alone in this. I know it, and you know it."

I responded with the same line as before:

"I did this all by myself."

I could see Mr. Rines losing patience with me because his face reddened—but I stuck to my guns. Even wild horses couldn't have dragged my partners' names out of me!

Mr. Rines leaned back in his chair and began staring at the wall behind me. It was like he was in a trance. I figured he was coming up with some plan to make me break the unwritten rule and give up the other guys' names.

Finally, he leaned forward and said, "All right, I think I'm going to call your parents about this." Calling my mother and father was the last thing I needed or wanted. And I must admit, when Mr. Rines told me he would call my parents, it put a little dent in my no-snitch armor!

Nonetheless, I responded to Mr. Rines by saying, "Go ahead and call my parents, but I will tell you the same thing; I did it alone."

I was acting cool and calm while I called his bluff, but, in reality, my heart was pounding so hard that it felt like it was coming out of my chest! Mr. Rines knew I was deathly afraid of my parents, but he figured I was willing to fall on my sword for this. My dad would think the situation was amusing until he discovered it might cost him money. My mother, on the other hand, wouldn't be so amused since she was the one who came to the school every time I got into trouble. The last time my mother came to my school, she'd promised to half-kill me if she ever had to come back because of my mischief. As I stated before, parents could get away with threats like that back then. Nowadays, you'd end up getting visited by child protection services.

Mr. Rines stared at the ceiling while rubbing his chin like he was in a trance again. After about 30 seconds, he looked at me and said, "Okay, mister. Since you did this all by yourself, you are going to pay back every penny of the interest you charged those students."

Now that got my attention! Since I had spent most of the money by then, I knew I was in hot water. And I knew that if my mother and father had to give me money, my name would be on a death warrant! I told Mr. Rines that I would pay the money back even though I had no clue how much it would cost.

"I know you will!" Mr. Rines responded, and then he told me to return to my classroom. As I entered through the classroom door, I could see the looks on my classmate's faces. Some of them had a look of shock on their faces as if they were surprised that I'd come back in one piece. Others just whispered and stared at me. Raymond, Tony, and Calvin had a look of worry on their faces. They feared that I spelled the beans and that they would join me on board this sinking ship.

But, after they found out that I never gave up their names, they all breathed a sigh of relief. I told them what happened and what I said in Mr. Rines's office. I also explained to them that I had to pay back all the interest accumulated for the invoices Mr. Lofton had retrieved from the floor. The problem was that, like me, they had already spent most of their share of the profits. Later that day, I discovered the interest was about $3.75. Therefore, all of us agreed to try to scrape up the money. And since it was the last week of school, time was of the essence. I went home that day and tried to find some money.

I asked my brother Micheal if he had any money to help me out, and after a long lecture on how that's what I deserved and how stupid I was, he finally reached into his pocket and handed me a dollar. "You better pay me back," he said. I told him I would, and then I left to find my two sisters, Debbie and Stephane.

I hoped that those two would give to save Aldric's behind fund. I asked Stephanie, and after I explained what happened, she stared at me with a *that's your problem* look on her face. But she and I were close, and she lent me twenty-five cents. Debbie was lying on her bed doing her homework and smiled when I asked her about lending me the money. She was amused with my story and why I needed the loan. As she turned over to begin studying again, she said, "Look on top of my dresser. There should be twenty or thirty cents on top." Thank the lord; it was thirty cents!

Debbie also had a departing word for me, "You better pay me back." I had scraped up $1.55, and with the seventy-five cents I had left from the bank profits, I was sitting on $2.30!

The following day I met with the guys, and we put all the money together to see how much we had scrapped up. I counted the money, and thank God we had $3.85! I entered the classroom and immediately walked to Mr. Lofton's desk. I told him that I had the money to pay everyone back.

"Well, that's great," he said with a slight smirk. He was enjoying every minute of the embarrassment this was causing me.

The class had not begun yet, so Mr. Lofton told me to go to the back of the room and move a desk away from the others so I could start the refunds. But, before I walked away from his desk, he handed me the bank receipts. As I sat at the desk, I looked around the classroom, and all eyes were on me.

I particularly noticed Raymond, Tony, and Calvin staring at me with a *better you than us* look on their faces. Mr. Lofton told the class, "If Aldric calls your name, you will walk back to his desk, and he will pay you the money he owes you."

As I called the names of the students I owed, a line began forming in front of my desk. I could hear laughter and whispering throughout the classroom. I was thinking, here I am, the big man and a prominent banker being the butt of all their jokes. If a student I owed wasn't in my class, I had to walk to their classroom to pay them. By then, I was the talk of the school. After all the students had been paid, I returned to my classroom. As soon as I walked in the door, Mr. Lofton asked me if I was finished refunding the money. I told him I was, and he told me to go to Mr. Rines's Office.

I arrived at the office, walked in the door, and the secretary asked me, "Can I help you?"

I answered. "Mr. Lofton said for me to come to see Mr. Rines."

The secretary opened Mr. Rines's door and said, "Mr.Rines, there's a young man out here to see you."

I heard Mr. Rines say, "Tell him to come in."

When I walked into his office, Mr. Rines "Oh, Aldric," he said. He pointed at a chair in front of his desk and said, "Sit down."

I sat down, and Mr. Rines leaned back in his chair and asked me,“"Did you pay back all the money”"

I answered, "Yes."

"Yes, what?"

"*Yes sir!*"

Mr. Rines asked me, "Have you learned anything from this experience?"

I thought about the question for a minute, then replied, "Well, the first thing I've learned is I shouldn't run a business that takes advantage of others."

"Anything else?" he asked, and I answered, "Yes."

Mr. Rines asked,"What else did you learn from this experience?"

"Well," I said, "the second thing that I learned is if you are going to run the kind of business that takes advantage of people, never keep records."

Mr. Rines's face turned red, and he yelled. "Get out of my office!"

I walked back to my classroom and sat down at my desk. Tony and Calvin walked over to me and asked, "What happened?" I told them what I said in the office, and they began to chuckle a little. After a few seconds, I began to chuckle too. Ultimately, the whole thing with the bank and how I was caught was amusing.

And as the years have gone by, it has become downright funny. The school week finally ended, and summer vacation had begun. That summer, my brother Michael and I worked for my father in his pulpwood business. The banker tag stuck with me all through high school. Guys would walk up to me and joke, saying, "There's the banker."

I would laugh and walk away while shaking my head. After graduation, I joined the United States Air Force but the passion for running a business still burned inside me. After my Air Force service, I married and had two beautiful daughters. I attended college and obtained my degree in Commercial Art & Graphic Design. I now run a graphics business along with two other companies. My daughters have given me three grandsons between the two of them. And now I'm happy and content.

Calvin moved up north; he now works in a factory. I don't talk to him much, but we are friends on Facebook.

Tony and Raymond both still live in North Carolina and are also working. I see them from time to time, and they always ask me if I remember when we ran that bank. We all laugh about it and talk about how much money we made. I'm still in awe that we almost got away with it. If it weren't for my mistake, we would have.

The seventies were a transitional time coming from civil rights and the turmoil of the sixties. But we all made the best we could of it. Although we were not rich, we had a happy childhood because we had our families and each other. I have seen some good and bad times throughout my life, and I have always tried to make the best out of what life has given me, good or bad.

I have faced many forms of bigotry and racism throughout my life. Even today, I face it while running my business. My father told me long ago that you get out of life what you put into it. My love for running a company gave me the strength to keep going despite what people say or do to me.

The childhood memories are stored in my mind's treasure chest, and I can access those memories anytime I want. Sometimes, when I hear an old song on the radio or see an old 70's TV show, it opens my treasure chest. And when that chest opens, I'm free to journey back in time. I'm free to think back to when Calvin, Tony, Raymond, and myself, Aldric, were little bankers.

Made in the USA
Columbia, SC
06 June 2023

17746766R00039